BOOK TITLE

5 SECRET OF DEFEATING DIVORCE

Table of contents

FORWARD

The author have strived to be as accurate and complete as possible in the creation of this report, You are encouraged to print this book for easy reading.

It has been theorized too many times that men and women are diametrically opposite beings. The theory goes on to say that there are totally different things that drive both these genders, and there are different things that they are looking for. That is the reason men and women act and behave in radically different ways.

Now, while the truth is that nature itself has ordained us to be different, which means our behaviors are characteristic of the gender that we belong to, it is also a sordid fact that this can create a lot of problems. There are several instances in which men and women do not understand each other, due to which there are disagreements and arguments between the two, even leading to drastic steps such as breakups and divorce.

I'll teach you the tried and true and proven techniques in this e-book which you are able to learn and employ immediately to better your love relationship and even your marriage!

Now I wish to tell you, yeah! You are able to take back the love of your life! Regardless how stubborn the opposition, regardless how far this individual might be from you, regardless how hopeless your state of affairs seems!

CHAPTER 1:

The Basics

SYNOPSIS

The intention of this eBook is to show what repairs could have been possible in relationships that soured down, and to reveal that with some more considerate effort, many of our relationships could be veered in the right direction.

This e-Book shows you that men and women are fundamentally different and we need to understand and accept these differences. We need to understand that there are different things that we look for in life, and even in a relationship, there are different things that a man and a woman look for in each other. If this one fundamental law of nature is kept in mind, then both genders would be able to live in better harmony with each other. Realizing our differences, we would be in better stead to become a unified whole.

THE BASICS

You should know that it takes time and it takes effort, but, most importantly, it takes a great deal of maturity and understanding. If we accept these differences in our partners, we will have more meaningful relationships. With this eBook, we are not trying to tell you to change what nature has made you as—that is not going to happen—but it is necessary to realize that your partner is a different person. It is not necessary that they should like the same things that you do and say the same things that you speak.

At the same time, most of the things that we label as selfish and inconsiderate in our partners, are actually quite different from what they appear. These things are nothing but the fundamental traits of those people. They are fashioned to behave in that particular manner. If a man forgets his wife's birthday, it is not because he does not care for her—it is because nature has designed him to focus on one job at a time.

Maybe he was just too busy with something else, his mind was biologically diverted to that task completely, and he slipped up. Or, when a woman spends too much time looking after herself, the man should not think that she is being vain. Nature has designed women in such a way that they like to take care of their appearance.

This is what we have to understand and accept. Instead of creating the world into a war zone full of enmity between

the sexes, it is important to understand the diametrical differences between the two genders, and live in harmony. We are designed to be different.
It is time to accept that and live in harmony.

In this eBook, you are going to see the different ways in which man and woman are designed to be different. You are going to read how to find out these differences in your partner and what you should do so that there is no cause for discord.

We will suggest you to maintain a journal of your relationship, a journal that you will create and update in discussion with your partner. You will be able to vent out your feelings in this journal and you will be able to understand how your partner is disposed as well. You will find that just the process of maintaining this journal will go a long way in helping your relationship to improve.

Really crucial and fundamental precepts you have to know first off if you truly, really, genuinely wish to win back the one you love and save your marriage!

- Mankind only wants what they don't actually have.

- Humans baulk matters which command or confine them.

- Humans love themselves to a higher degree than anything else.

In the first place, you have to learn and remember the above really crucial precepts regarding mortal nature. To a certain extent, these precepts apply to everybody, including you and me!

Really crucial things you must not do if you earnestly wish to recover your mate or save your marriage don't show that you're starving for your spouse's or mate's presence.

Regardless how much you wish your mate or your spouse to remain by your side, or to be back with you, more starving and hanging on will only make that individual even more tired and fed up with seeing you or making up with you.

Rather, cultivate the mental attitude, habit and conduct such that you don't require that individual to be around for your happiness or pleasure. You truly don't require someone else's presence or approval to receive happiness and peacefulness.

If you discover how to cultivate this sort of mental attitude and habit, you'll discover that your mate will be the one who will become frightened! They will get frightened of losing you!
Think of this: human beings tend to want what they don't actually have!

If your mate or spouse is seeing somebody other than you, don't stop them from seeing other people! Have a competitor around?

Here's what you have to do. Don't stop your mate from seeing others. If you sound off, and whine, and nag, I can tell you, the more they'll wish to see the other individual!

How come? They can't stand your sounding off, and yammering, and nagging! If you wish to stop them from having something that they desire, all the more they'll desire it! Humans tend to desire what they don't actually have.

So, if you attempt to stop them seeing a different individual, all the more they'll wish to be with that individual! To them, it'll be a great challenge if you attempt to stop them.

If they ever win that individual, they'll feel triumphant about it! And guess what, you're the one challenging them that they won't have what they desire! Remember, battling to get back the one you love almost guarantees your failure.

So, what you have got to do is to provide them freedom of choice! Let them feel that you're the better individual to be around than your competition because you respect their freedom and their options!

Don't restrict your mate or your spouse. Human beings tend to baulk things or individuals who command or confine them!

Respect your mate's decisions or wishes to do whatsoever he/she wishes to do during a specific day or during a specific time.

If he/she wishes to go out with someone else today, let them alone! If he/she doesn't wish to see you today, let them go!

The more you don't give them your tending, guess what, they'll want your tending back! They'll begin wanting it! And they'll urgently want it back.

The more you provide them attention, the more they'll feel that you wish to command them, to restrict them, and the result is, they'll baulk it, they'll battle back! This will just hurt the relationship between the 2 of you.

CHAPTER 2:

Then And Now

SYNOPSIS

Very few people may be totally happy with their lives today. Surely, most lives today are shrouded by problems such as distrust among the partners, disagreements over slight issues, suspicions, ill will and even hatred. Relationships are continually souring all around us, and most times, we feel that nothing can be done about it. We resign ourselves by saying that it was meant to be that way.

Life was completely different in the good old times, at least on the face of it. We weren't so technologically advanced back then and maybe we gave more importance to our human relationships than we do today. Man needed woman and woman needed man more than they do today—that is a fact.

THE VIEW

The shapes our relationships are taking right now are downright deplorable. 1 in 2 couples are ending up in a breakup or a divorce. The levels of animosity are definitely rising, and this is certainly no good.

Why is this happening? What is it that we are failing to see? Despite making a diehard commitment at the start of our relationship, in the heydays as you may call them, what happens that makes the relationship so drastically irreparable?

Certainly, the problem lies in one of the partners or both. There are some very basic things that we are completely missing out on. We are not spending the time to realize that men and women are totally different kinds of beings, and that the only way to live successfully in harmony is by understanding each other completely.

If you think that is too difficult to achieve, you need to think again. You need to see that the situation is not all that bleak as it seems. There is just one link in this chain, one single strand, that we are missing out on. If we simply see this one missing link and accept it, we will be able to do much better with our lives.

That is what it is all about—mutual understanding and acceptance.

That is what we need to learn.

And, yes, in this chapter, we begin creating the journal of your relationships that will help save your rocking relationship boat. This is your reference point and your guide, the place where you find your fumbling relationship begin to take root once again.

We see this very common scenario in the world around us today... maybe in our own lives too.

It is someone's wedding day. They look into each other's eyes and vow to be together "until death do them part". Standing in front of the marriage celebrant it is difficult to imagine how the two could ever not feel so in love as they do today.

Yet 5, 10, 15 years later they are standing in front of a judge and this time they are told they are divorced. It is not exactly the fairy tale ending they had anticipated all those years ago.

This scenario is a reality for over 50% of couples who marry. While the length of the relationship may be different among couples, and there are other reasons for the divorce, the reality is, over half of all marriages will end in divorce. The statistics are worse for remarriages.

It is a gloomy picture, and perhaps you are feeling depressed wondering what hope your marriage or relationship has in the face of such statistics. The great thing about statistics is that there are good as well as bad statistics and other statistics reveal that if a couple can work through the problems in their relationship; they can potentially bond stronger than ever and go on to have an even better relationship.

Why is all this happening? Ultimately, it is our perceptions of what makes a good relationship and our expectations of our partner, which creates the friction in marriage.

As we learn to understand why we have these expectations and how to challenge with them, we can look at our relationships with new eyes and appreciate them for what they are, rather than for what they are not, With this knowledge, all relationships potentially can move forward.

Our ability to relate to each other has evolved over our lifetime. We learn by observing the culture we grew up in and through our life experiences. As children, we watch our parents and we see how they relate with each other.

We interact with our siblings and this contributes to our knowledge of how people in close relationships interact with each other. We learn from talking to our friends and often compare and contrast their experiences with our own. As we reflect on what shapes the way we interact with others and why it does this, we find the key to beginning the restoration of a successful relationship.

Here are a couple of practical steps that may help the process. Try to do them together as a couple.

Reflect on who you are and what has shaped your thoughts on life and relationships. Take a day or two to really think deeply about this and ask your partner the same questions. Compare their thoughts with yours.

Use a journal to write down significant events in your relationship each day and what experiences caused them to occur and what your expectations were that caused that let down. These events go a long way in reinforcing your relationships. Even as you feel that you are drifting apart, if you just happen to read about these events in your journal, you will reminisce about those happy days you had together and perhaps you will have a change of heart. You will make an effort to patch up the relationship again. You will want to be together again to relive those happy days, and somewhere deep inside, you will get the confidence that the situation is not as bleak as it appears on the outside.

Chances are that your partner is reconsidering as well. Since the love you started out with was quite strong and determined, your partner is not going to want to peter it down too. Sit together and think. Maybe a solution will emerge out of the entire morass. Maybe you will want to be together for life once again, just as you committed to each other during those marriage.

But times have changed. We have become more mechanical, more materialistic. Our lives aren't as simple as they were before. Our obligations of the day aren't divided simply into work-time and family-time. Many more things vie for our attention each day.

Still, the basic rules that were established back then are still quite prevalent. Gender roles were assigned to man and woman back then, all those centuries ago, and they still remain. Woman lib regardless, there are still gender roles that are prevalent. And this is more commonly seen when people are in a relationship.

Until recently, humans traditionally mated for life with one and sometimes in polygamous societies a number of mates. Fifty years ago when people divorced, they often faced accusations and lost lifelong friendships. Today, it is likely that many of those in our circle of friends are divorced and may even have remarried with new partners.

If we look back even further to the days when our ancestors were hunters and gatherers, we see a completely different situation than what is the reality for most couples today. History has shown us that our ancestors were a mainly hunting and gathering society. Men would go and hunt for food while women collected mainly seeds and berries around their home.

They relied on each other for the provision of everything material, but for the most part, they did not receive a lot of direct emotional support from each other. Instead, men developed camaraderie with the men they hunted with, while the women spent most of the time with each other, helping look after children and prepare the food. Women usually found the emotional support they needed with the women they worked with each day.

This pattern continued until the 20th century. Although the type of work that men and women undertook changed drastically, the gender roles remained much the same. The man would go out to work and the woman would stay at home. This scenario is not only typically true of a "western" culture; studies of most world cultures reveal similar trends.

During the 20th century, traditional roles began to change. Perhaps the world wars created a need for women to work outside the home, but women started to take on traditionally male jobs. In some situations, women earned more money than men did. Some men even began to stay at home and look after the children. Traditional gender roles began to change, women lobbied for equal rights and in a few cases, men began choosing to stay home, care for their children and home while their wife worked.

The reaction of men and women to this trend is food for countless books and audio talks on how this transition has affected the way men and women relate to each other. The common theme that appears to be emerging from all studies and research is that men will be men and women will be women.

It appears that no matter how much society is evolving, some things remain the same. There is a consistency in the way men look at situations and deal with them and the way that women look at situations and deal with them. The gender specific needs of both men and women have changed little from the time of our ancestors and most problems arise when those needs neglected Controversial thoughts they may seem to be, but important to think about nonetheless.

You and your partner may like to reflect on this thought in your journals. Knowing how to identify and meet your personal own needs is the first step in healing a broken relationship.

CHAPTER 3:

Know The Differences

SYNOPSIS

There is a constant power struggle between the two human genders on this planet. This is not different from a competition, in which each gender wants to impress upon the other that they are better than the other.

Men and women comprehend emotion, communicating, sexuality, faithfulness, work and income because of the way they were socialized and because they've been influenced by their own parents' perceptual experience. They bring in these ideas to the marriage and therefore have their own baggage of notions regarding what is passable and intolerable in a union, what they have to provide their mate and what to anticipate in return

This is definitely a very sorry state of affairs. If, instead of all these discords, the two genders would live together in harmony, the world would become a more harmonious place.

THE DIFFERENCES

Women attack love as informed consumers...they kick the tires, see under the hood, run the engine, check out the mileage. Women enjoy love, however being practical-minded, not enough to ignore likely shortcomings. Handsomeness and romantic love interest a woman, but in thinking about likely suitors, a woman likewise views the practical, like a wooer's economical prospect, emotional stableness, trustworthiness, and what sort of father he will be.

In spite of a reputation for practicality, male persons come away as hopeless romantics. They're much more prone to fall topsy-turvily in love and likewise more prone to idealize the target of their fondness.

If the bodywork is great and the grillwork pretty, frequently a man will purchase on-the-scene, no questions asked. It requires practice to learn that gender differences don't represent menaces to a marriage, merely a cause for celebration and a chance to enlarge a person's area of experience.

Attempt to remember that your mate isn't your reflection. In a loving, good partnership, individualism and separateness are wholesome concepts that each mate must work on.

Don't sweat the little stuff is likely one advice that doesn't forever work for marriage, as it's crucial to observe the little stuff, if the marriage were to thrive. Most of the true work in relationships is coming about in more hushed moments in littler spaces.
Illustrations would be:

- Putting off bringing up the bad garage door while your hubby is rushing to meet a deadline and has to center on his project for a couple of hours.
- Assisting the youngsters and keeping them away from the kitchen while your wife fixes supper.
- Offering to collect your hubby's shirts at the cleaners as he forgot to do it yesterday.
- Filling the car tank if you know that your hubby has to go out of town on a customer visit.
- taking your wife dancing as she's always loved to dance even if you've 2 left feet and have always despised it.

One thorn in a marriage is income. Chances are married persons have their own ways of spending and laying aside income. If both hubby and wife earn like wages, agree on how to break up the home expenses before marrying so no one feels betrayed or deprived financially.

While it was all right to expect him to pay for supper and the film while you were going out, marriage calls for a real economic partnership. Or, if you understand that your hubby is especially

averse to worthless shopping flings, make an attempt to cut down your buying trips and center on the necessities rather than on your impulses.

Don't forget to talk about your investing preferences and attempt to stick with a budget and a savings plan.

Work at keeping your partner perked up intellectually. If there's anything that grinds, it's a wife who perpetually discusses what's on sale and a hubby who knows zip but what teams made it to the playoffs this year. Retrospect to courtship days when both of you could talk till the wee hours of the morning as you were intrigued with what each of you performed in the office that day, in that book or film etc.

Enrich one another with your lives and vicarious experiences. Let the other know that you've a pursuit in life and what it has to provide, and make every effort not to be a dull spouse by reading more, trying out more, and living more.

A lot of individuals state that youngsters put a damper on the union. Who has time for passion and love when the youngsters are screaming their lungs out or running a one hundred five degree fever?
Or when income has to be scrounged up to pay for teeth?

Raising kids may turn us into impatient, stressed-out organisms so if engaging a sitter overnight won't interrupt the monthly budget, do so and vanish – just the 2 of you. But don't utilize that time away from youngsters to sound off about each other's habits or to bring up past incidents! Rather than viewing marriage blessed with elevated points or fraught with crushed points, think about it instead as a series of landmarks.

Landmarks have to be viewed as chances to make a union stronger and more fulfilling. These landmarks become clear at mid-life where couples have formulated a greater sense of time limits and an urgency in their want to make the most out of their union and their lives. The mid-life years are an innate time for contemplations: couples now have the benefit of being able to see where they've been, where they are and where they wish to go.

Provide credit where it's due, be generous with regard and be sincere in your praise. Do you occasionally discover yourself wishing that your mate would compliment you? A lot of couples find that as they settle into their union, the regard or kind praises are not as frequent as when they were going out. Giving credit where it's due and becoming sincere about your praises goes a long way toward reinforcing health in a marriage.

If you discover that your wife works religiously on the treadmill to avoid the weight, did you ever think that she's likely doing this to please you? Stating something like, "You're so disciplined in your attempts to accomplish your goals, I'm proud of you" will add to her self-assurance and reinforce her position that she's doing something that's fit and that you value.

If your hubby is great at crunching numbers, praise him for his accomplishments at speedy calculation. "You're astonishing with numbers" will give him a feel of pride, and he will feel significant to you. Without doubt a lot of authorities and marriage counselors will differ in opinion on how to save a marriage, but they all agree on the following fundamental Components of a solid marriage – only the words and the way they're conveyed are dissimilar.

We Are Deigned to Be Different!

Men and women have been compared to being residents of two different planets in a popular series of books currently on the market. The hypothesis of the author is that despite popular, modern thinking men and women really are different. In fact, they do have a predisposition to think and act in a different way depending on whether we are male or female.

This is because men and women really are made differently! Some of the arguments that occur within a relationship are the result of neither member of the couple grasping this fact. Without being too technical, the practical outcomes of these differences mean that men and women respond differently to the same situation.

This is not because either member is uncaring, or forgetful or in some way not responding to the needs of their partner, it simply means that in many cases they are incapable of being any different, simply because this is a gender specific situation and not a personal one.

Where the Power Struggle Begins and How to End It

Understanding that a man will always want to solve a problem rather than talk about it and a woman will always want to talk it out in order to solve it is important. Women often complain men don't want to listen to them talk about their problems, while their silent partners often wish that women would stop talking about the problem so they can solve it.

The design of the male brain is specialized to focus on one job at a time and to do that job well. The nervous system in his brain is "wired" so that he can see a problem, work out how to fix the problem and then to fix it. His brain provides a man with the ability to think analytically, to work well with numbers and generally to complete complex tasks.

Women on the other hand, have a brain that is "wired" to multitask well. Women tend to be able to do the washing, cook the dinner, and look after the children at the same time.

When a woman asks her husband to do something while his mind is preoccupied and his focus is elsewhere at the time, he is inclined to forget her request, but this is completely unintentional on his part. He really did forget, not because he does not love her enough to carry out the request, but because his focus was in doing something else at the time, she made the request.

Understanding that there are important physiological differences (and hormonal ones) that drive the behavior of men and women is an important step in understanding that our partners failure to meet our expectations are often unintentional. Once we can accept that, we can view the actions of our partners from another perspective.

For Your Journals

Discuss a recent misunderstanding you and your partner had with each other. Write about the differences between men and women and think about how your partner's actions in that situation that upset you may have been typical of the differences between genders rather

than something personal they are "doing wrong".

CHAPTER 4:

Control Your Tongue

SYNOPSIS

Things you utterly must not state if you truly wish to change the mind of your mate.

WATCH WHAT YOU SAY

If you wish to change the mind of your spouse or mate concerning anything, you have to not say "But I love you..." I can tell you, stating that

and stressing how much you love them isn't going to get them to change their mind.

When you state "But I love you..." you are in reality telling your mate that you wish him/her to do something your style! Not his/her style.

Recall that "human beings tend to love themselves to a higher degree than anything else!" When you state "I love you..." you are in reality loving yourself more. You wish your spouse to do things which will gratify your ego, thus you wish your spouse to do things your way. And your spouse recognizes it! He/She is not going to alter his/her mind simply because you tell them "I love you..."

If you wish your spouse to do particular things your way, you have to not say to your partner "But I've done this and this for you..."

Prevent stirring up the past about what you've done for him

or her. The past is already deceased. Stressing how much you've done for your spouse will only tell him/her that he/she has to do stuff your way because that's the price they have to ante up for all that you've helped them do in the past.

The more you state this, the more your mate will wish to drift apart from you or leave you. He or she will be too frightened to be with you as they know their motion is restricted by how much they may repay you.
So, at any expense, prevent giving them the feeling that they have to ante up a price simply to be with you! No one on this Earth likes to be commanded or restricted by another individual!

Prevent stating things like "But it's your duty...."

Your mate won't like to be tied down by duty or obligations. When it bears on relationship, there can be rules. Love is unconditional.
By

Stressing too much on duty, you're going to turn your mate off.

He or she won't desire to be with someone who wishes to impose rules and ordinances on them. So, it is your job and obligation to see that you give your spouse no excuse to leave you for some other individual.

So, what precisely must you say if you wish to alter the mind of your spouse to make them accomplish things your way, or view things your way?

First of all, stress the strong points if they view things your way. Let them recognize the Advantages and benefits of executing and viewing things your way. Provide them clear-cut explanations.

Second, remember your mate isn't concerned about what other people want. He or she isn't worried about what you wish. He/she is more interested in what he/she wants and what he/she may receive. A lot of times, they're not against your thoughts, or whatever it is you need, but they're really against your pushing aside their freedom of choice.

So, provide them what they desire. Provide them freedom of choice. Let them know they've the freedom to choose what they wish to believe in or what they don't wish to believe in. And let them know they've the freedom to decide what they wish to do, and what they wish not to do.

The magic words you are able to tell them are “Yes! I comprehend what you're saying. Why don't you try it /do it...”

“Yes” is the magic word which unites you and your partner right away.

“I comprehend...” demonstrates you're with your partner, you're hearing them out, and you honor their decision.

“Why don't you try it / do it ...” tells them you back their decision or choice, even though you're not in favor of it.
If you've a competitor, always remember, the individual who may give your mate more freedom of choice will most likely be the one your mate wishes to be with most.

If you bear all the above precepts in mind, you're likely to have more success in altering your mates mind and make them accomplish things your way.

CHAPTER 5:

Growing

SYNOPSIS

We surely don't divorce our friends just because of a misinterpretation, so if we addressed our spouse as a dear friend, we likely won't ever require a divorce lawyer and carry out the awful exercise of divorce. Friends are evermore. Even if we move out of town or adopt residence abroad, we preserve our friendship.

There is solid biological evidence in what we say—the difference between man and woman is not just a matter of conjecture; there is an actual hormonal reason for it. While men are driven by the robust testosterone hormone—a hormone that creates a kind of an aggressive edge—women are governed by the milder oxytocin hormone, which compels them to give and receive love and care.

So, it is not just a superficial difference that the two sexes on this planet have. There is much more. The difference runs deep inside; it deals with the hormonal composition of the two genders. That's what makes us to different.

If we want to survive on this planet, we will hardly be able to do it by living in isolation and thinking about our own selfish interests.

TRANSFORMATION

Situations that at one stage would have been perhaps overlooked are now added to the list of things that the partner is doing wrong. When two people in a relationship are under stress, little things often become major issues. Once a relationship reaches this point, it is very difficult for one or both partners to see the good things their partner can offer them and the relationship.

Men and women are driven by their hormones. Testosterone the male sex hormone, and oxytocin, the female sex hormone each playextremely important roles in the way men and women act and react. Testosterone plants a desire in men to protect and provide for their wives. Oxytocin produces a strong need in women to nurture and care for others.

Adequate levels of both hormones are essential to produce a feeling of wellbeing and contentment. When both partners have high hormonal levels, they deal with life and their relationships in a positive way. When the hormonal levels are diminished, stress levels are raised, leading to greater risk of conflict within the relationship.

When couples had defined roles, it was easy for the couple to live their lives with these hormones operating naturally. The man in the relationship would go to work and earn enough money to sustain his family with a suitable lifestyle and all their needs. The woman in the relationship would stay home and care for her family. When couples are in a good relationship and understanding and responding to each other's needs physically, emotionally and socially, these hormones are produced in increasing quantities.

Society and circumstances has change the way we do things. Often, the man is no longer the sole provider and his wife may have a job, and yet still feel the need to nurture and care for her family. Both of these situations create tension. The man no longer feels his wife has the same need for his provision, something that would drive him to succeed in the past. The woman feels frustrated she still often has to go home and do much of the work around the house because her husband seems to prefer to go home and sit and read the newspaper or watch the television.

Testosterone and oxytocin are produced differently in each partner and once couples understand this, it will help change the way they view this scenario. In this scenario, each member of the couple is instinctively doing what is necessary for them to restore their hormonal levels. At the end of the day, both have returned home with depleted hormonal levels. To raise her levels the woman needs to nurture and care, and give and receive love to stimulate oxytocin production. Relaxation is his way of increasing his hormonal levels.

Spend some time reflecting on all your partner's positive qualities. Write them down in your journal and take some time every day to read them and reflect how much your partner adds to your life.

Read more about the way our hormones influence our actions and reflect on this in your journal.

Since love is less lasting and friendship more long-lasting, every endeavor must be made to make our mate isn't only a lover and a partner, but as well a friend. Friendship is observable manifestation of matureness. Marriage is a duty larger than life, and may be a source of bother or sound joy. Only if we turn those bothers and joys into building blocks for a lasting friendship may we say that we've taken the firm path to a union made in heaven.

If there's true friendship between hubby and wife, the marriage avoids ending up on the rocks. Rather it becomes a rock-hard marriage where no person or condition may put it asunder.

Friendship in a union means that the union will be significant with memories of laughter and wit, for didn't we pick those friends who made us laugh the most? Friendship likewise means open and honest communicating; a no holds barred type of coupling where our comfort level with our mate goes beyond a hundred percent, guaranteed that what we state and how we say it won't be labeled or taken in a damaging light.

Friendship between couples returns wholesome feelings of good will and faithfulness. Our spouse – our friend – has our concerns at heart, won't cheat on us and will be our most steadfast supporter.

Friendship likewise makes mates stronger; this durability is reinforced by the pleasure of shared history, of nostalgia and designs for the future.

Romance is a great thing, and we may utilize heaps of it when our relationships get rough. But mature friends are cognizant that romance maybe a roadblock to friendship. How come? As romance blots out the darker side of our being – our concerns, anxieties, and insecurities. Yet, it's those fears, anxieties and insecurities that by nature draw us to our friend.

Familiarity doesn't spawn contempt. It spawns content. A sense of contentment corresponds with satisfaction, warmth, and firm assurance. Partaking in a life together in love and friendship makes for a book that's deeper and denser in shared histories, in content.

If you were to ask a content bachelor and a jubilantly married man to each author their stories, you'd get a favorable narration from both. The single individual's position would however be I, me and myself – and perhaps a string of blind dates and Saturday nights alone. The husband will discuss "us", of mutual interests – a story decidedly made richer as there are two stories, not one.

Much as it sounds awfully passé, marriage is a commitment, and people have to make every attempt not to degrade that commitment in any way. Remaining married is a lifelong, missionary-like enterprise. It calls for guts. It calls for nerves of steel to make a union work. A sense of humor and a humbler degree of egotism may sustain us in that work.

The obstructions will be many, and there will be spots where we'll question our saneness, uncertain if we may truly hang in there.
It will be a massive effort to stay attracted to the same qualities that pulled you to your spouse on the first day you got together. Your spouse is yet the same individual you fell in love with, he hasn't altered his soul, his being, only his closet.

CONCLUSION

So if there's merely one way to divorce, but a 1000 ways to save your union, which route will you choose? Are you going to quit or accept one more hurdle?

We hope you've enjoyed this e-Book and will apply some of the tips given·

www.ingramcontent.com/pod-product-compliance
Lightning Source LLC
LaVergne TN
LVHW040932150826
845672LV00007B/2326

* 9 7 9 8 8 4 6 7 9 8 9 6 0 *